D0282804

Soul Searching Journal

A Guide to Self-Discovery for Girls

WRITTEN BY *Sarah Stillman*

ILLUSTRATED BY SUSAN GROSS

BEYOND WORDS Publishing INC

Published by
Beyond Words Publishing, Inc.
20827 NW Cornell Road, Suite 500
Hillsboro, Oregon 97124
503-531-8700

The information contained in this journal is intended to be educational and not for diagnosis, prescription, or treatment of mental and/or physical health disorders, whatsoever. This information should not replace competent medical and/or psychological care. The authors and publisher are in no way liable for any use or misuse of the information.

ISBN: 1-58270-056-7

Editors: Barbara Mann, Emily Strelow, Megan Roseman,
Carol Grimes, and Corey Mistretta
Design: Andrea Boven / Boven Design Studio, Inc.
Proofreader: Susan Beal

Printed in the United States of America
Distributed to the book trade by Publishers Group West

LIBRARY OF CONGRESS CATALOGING-IN-PUBLICATION DATA

Stillman, Sarah, 1984-
    Soul searching journal : a guide to self-discovery for girls / written by Sarah Stillman ; illustrated by Susan Gross.
        p. cm.
    ISBN 1-58270-056-7 (hardcover)
    1. Girls—Conduct of life—Juvenile literature. 2. Spiritual life—Juvenile literature. [1. Self-evaluation. 2. Conduct of life. 3. Youths' writings.] I. Gross, Susan, 1960- ill. II. Title.

BJ1651 .S854 2001
158'.0835'2—dc21   00-068031

The corporate mission of Beyond Words Publishing, Inc:
Inspire to Integrity

What is the Soul Searching Journal?

Somewhere deep inside, we all know what's best for us—it's only a matter of listening. *The Soul Searching Journal* is about tuning into your own inner wisdom and by doing so, discovering more about yourself. There are plenty of activities in this journal to put you on the path to self-discovery, but keep in mind that these are suggestions—nothing about journaling is set in stone. You can use this journal to channel your creativity, sort out problems, or make sense out of life—whatever *you* want. The more you write, the more you'll love it and the more you'll discover about yourself!

Important Tips to Remember

Although the first rule in journaling is that there are no rules, here are some suggestions to keep in mind as you begin the *Soul Searching Journal*:

⊙ Your journal is for you! You don't have to share it with anyone unless you choose to.

⊙ Don't censor yourself. Write what you feel, not what you think you should be feeling or wish you were feeling. There is no need to sound cool, sophisticated, or intelligent when you are writing in your private journal.

⊙ Don't worry about grammar or spelling. It's fine to make these types of mistakes, since your English teacher isn't looking over your shoulder and shaking her head. Focus on self-expression, not grammar.

Remembering Your Dreams

Dreams are windows into our souls, and they have important messages for us. As soon

as you wake up in the morning, try to remember your dreams. Write down detailed

descriptions of where you were, what you felt, and what you saw/smelled/heard/

said/did. Record how you feel about the dream and then date each dream, so that you can look back on it and remember when it occurred. Don't miss out on the brilliant ideas your subconscious creates during sleep!

Dream *Interpretation*

After writing down the narrative of a dream, try to understand what it might symbolize. To decode your dream, begin by recording the emotions you experienced during and after it. Think about the meaning of your actions, the colors or people you saw. Then, write down anything in real life that you think the dream might relate to.

Write a "Me List"

This is a list of 100 adjectives that describe you. Yes, 100! Why so many? Well, the first few you write will probably be the generic things you've always considered yourself to be: talkative or shy, athletic or klutzy. Get past these words that have always labeled you. Once you've reached number 50 or so, your mind will be challenged to dig deeper. You will learn even more about yourself.

Deconstruct Your *Myths*

We all have myths about ourselves. Sometimes we are the ones who create these myths; other times we let the people around us dictate who we are and where our talents lie. What are the myths that surround your identity? Label them, and give reasons why they aren't true. Figuring out our myths is the first step to dispelling them.

Color *Your Mood*

Colors are often overlooked as a useful and influential aspect of our lives. The colors around us can really affect our feelings. Write down the colors that affect you most. What colors are you most drawn to? Cut out samples of these colors from magazines or fabrics, or use paints and color pencils. How does each color affect your mood?

Smells

"Stop and smell the roses" is excellent advice. Pay attention to the smells of your life: flowers, shampoo, grass, cookies, whatever surrounds you. The smells you love are a part of who you are. Spray your favorite perfume or dab some essential oil on these pages. Use a sprig of dried rosemary or lavender as a bookmark for your journal. Write down the smells that affect you most. What memories do they conjure up?

Brat Page

Here's a place to vent all that you're feeling, no matter how ridiculous or selfish it may be. When you've had some time to gain some perspective, return to this page. Do you feel any differently?

Tales of
Traveling

These pages are for writing about the places you visit or wish to visit, the people you meet, and what you learn from your travels. Paste down any memorabilia from your trip like airplane tickets, photos, or postcards.

"*Bits & Pieces*"
Collect the

This is a place for the tidbits of life. Write down that hilarious joke your best friend whispered to you during the school assembly. Photocopy that inspiring quote or poem in your English book. Cut out that picture in National Geographic. Express yourself through different textures and images. These "bits and pieces" can form a collage of your experiences, memories and thoughts.

Magic
Potion

Imagine that you will be offered a magic potion that allows you to change one thing about yourself. Will you decide to take it? If so, what will you change?

Body
Beautiful

As feminist Gloria Steinem once wrote, "If we bless our bodies, they will bless us." Listening to your body and learning to honor and love it is a crucial part of soul searching. What are some of the positive things your body does for you? What are some ways to pamper your body?

Don't Ignore Your Emotions

Instead of ignoring the powerful things you feel each day, try closely monitoring your emotions. The more you follow what's going on inside your head, the more in control you will feel. Write about the last time you cried or felt strong emotion. When was it, and why? What was the result of expressing your emotions? Do you feel better, or worse?

Discover *Inner Joy*

What makes you happy?
Sometimes it's easy to lose
track of the things we
cherish in life. Try not only
to list the things you love,
but also why you love them.
Collage pictures of your
favorite foods, people,
places—anything that
makes you smile!

Question *Your World*

Write a question at the top of the page. You might ask yourself anything from "Is there a God?" to "How can I improve my relationship with my parents?" Then, try to answer your question. It may help to approach the problem with several different answers. You don't have to decide on a definite answer, just consider the possibilities.

Switch It Up

The human brain is divided into two halves: the analytical, mathematical *left* brain, and the creative, emotional *right* brain. Although the right side of your brain is responsible for lots of cool and creative stuff, most people don't use it as much as they should. To get your right side of your brain working, write a journal entry with your non-dominant hand (if you're right-handed use your left, and vice versa). You may be surprised at what the other side of your brain has to say.

Get *Inspired!*

This is a place to collect anything that fires up the artist within you. Write down ideas for a story, a poem, a painting, or whatever else inspires you. These pages will be very helpful the next time your creative well runs dry.

Rocky
Relationships

Think about a relationship you want to understand better. Write about a key incident in that relationship. How does that person make you feel when you are around him/her? Why? In a perfect world, how would your relationship be different?

What Are Your Passions?

So, what are you passionate about? What do you love doing? What jobs intrigue you? Think about how you feel when you're doing something you really like. This is an important key to who you are. Take a moment to brainstorm and write down your passions. Some people immediately know their passions, but with others it takes lots of time, patience, and thought.

Simple
Solutions

Think of a problem, situation, or event that frustrates or confuses you. Then start writing your emotions, feelings, and fears about it. Really analyze how you are feeling and why you feel that way. If you could change anything, what would it be?

Skeletons
in the Closet

Spend a moment thinking about your deepest secrets. Since we can't escape from our own secrets, we might as well use them as tools for growth. Reflect upon how your secrets shape you as a human being. Take some time to open the closet of skeletons and dust them off. Why do you hide the things you do? What makes your secrets so mortifying? Do you have any secrets from yourself?

Your Ideal World

A wonderful way to get ideas on how to help the world is to think about what your perfect vision of this Earth would be like. Make a list of things you'd want in your ideal world. When you're done brainstorming, take a look at your list and pick one item that particularly compels you. How could you get involved and begin making a difference? What can you do right at this moment to help?

Create a
Self~Portrait

Use colored pencils, crayons, fabric, glitter, and whatever else you can think of to create a self-portrait. Then surround your self-portrait with pictures, words, or objects that you like. Look at it when you are done. What does your self-portrait tell you about yourself? Everyone is a collage made up of the different ideas we have, the people who surround us, the places we've been, and the things we believe in.

Myths

Reality
Check

Take all the negative and
unhealthy images you see in
the media, things that you
don't think are true about
yourself or other girls and put
them under "Myths." Then
take all the positive and
healthy media images of girls
and women and paste them
under "Reality Check."

Celebrate *Yourself*

Have you noticed how easily the average human mind can create negative thoughts and images? That's where affirmations come to the rescue. Affirmations are short sentences that state a positive fact about our lives, or at least something we desire to be true. They shower us with optimism and poise by exchanging destructive thoughts for constructive ones. Write down your affirmations here.

The Anti-You

In figuring out who we are, it can be surprisingly helpful to figure out who we are not. In your journal, create a character that is the absolute opposite of you. Think about how she (or he? or it?) looks, sounds, and acts. Imagine a day in which she mingles with your family, talks to your teachers, and has a sleepover with your friends. What is her day like? Why is she so different from you? When you're done, reflect on this new character you've created. Maybe even write a story about her or draw a picture. Your feelings about the Anti-You can shed light upon the traits you possess, both positive and negative.

What's Your *Philosophy?*

We are responsible for deciding how to think, what to believe, and how to handle each opportunity that comes our way. What's your personal philosophy? Which beliefs do you have that are different from your friends or family? Which are the same? Why?

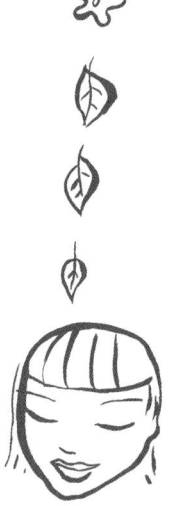

Your Personal Mission Statement

What exactly does a personal mission statement consist of? Some people write just a sentence or two, others write a paragraph, a page, or a list that outlines their personal goals and beliefs. You can quote a favorite author, philosopher, or song. Ask your parents and friends if they've ever used mission statements in their lives. If all else fails, just sit down and write whatever comes into your head. When your statement is complete, look at it whenever you need inspiration.

Write a
Letter to Yourself

Once a year, on a special occasion such as your birthday, write a letter to yourself. In this letter, you can reflect on the past year, state your goals for the coming year, and simply remind yourself of who you really are and want to be. A year later, read your letter and write a new one.

Accomplish it All

Write down all the things that you want to do in your life. Don't worry if they seem too big or even impossible. Remember, anything can be accomplished if you put your mind to it.